LEWIS & CLARK

Jill K. Mulhall, M.Ed.

Contributing Author

Wendy Conklin, M.A.

Consultants

Vanessa Ann Gunther, Ph.D.
Department of History
Chapman University

Nicholas Baker, Ed.D.
Supervisor of Curriculum and Instruction
Colonial School District, DE

Katie Blomquist, Ed.S.
Fairfax County Public Schools

Publishing Credits

Rachelle Cracchiolo, M.S.Ed., *Publisher*
Conni Medina, M.A.Ed., *Managing Editor*
Emily R. Smith, M.A.Ed., *Series Developer*
Diana Kenney, M.A.Ed., NBCT, *Content Director*
Courtney Patterson, *Senior Graphic Designer*
Lynette Ordoñez, *Editor*

Image Credits: Cover and pp. 1, 18 (top), 23 (top), 25 (bottom), 31 Granger, NYC; p. 4 Rembrandt Peale/ZUMA Press/Newscom; p. 5 Sarin Images/Granger, NYC; pp. 6, back cover NativeStock/North Wind Picture Archives; p. 7 Courtesy of the Montana Historical Society, Don Beatty, photographer; p. 8 NARA [300353]; p. 9 (bottom) Illustration by Ed Vebell/Getty Images; pp. , 9, 11, 12, 16, , 26, 27 North Wind Picture Archives; p. 11 (top) Leavenworth/Kansas City/Atchison, KS Signature Event - "A Journey Forth"; pp. 12-13 Creative Commons Gooseterrain2, used under CC BY-SA 3.0; p. 13 LC [mtj-mtjbib014558]; p. 14 Michael Haynes; p. 15 Bettmann/Getty Images; p. 17 (front) Witold Skrypczak/Alamy Stock Photo, (back) Unknown/Alamy Stock Photo; p. 18 (middle) Lowell Georgia/Getty Images; p. 21 Russ Bishop Photography/Newscom; p. 24 Bill Grant/Alamy Stock Photo; p. 25 (top) Bill Grant/Alamy Stock Photo, (middle) Ken Welsh/Bridgeman Images; p. 32 NARA [300353]; all other images from iStock and/or Shutterstock.

Library of Congress Cataloging-in-Publication Data

Names: Mulhall, Jill K., author.
Title: Lewis & Clark / Jill K. Mulhall.
Description: Huntington Beach, CA : Teacher Created Materials, 2017. | Includes index. | Audience: Grades 4-6.
Identifiers: LCCN 2016034227 (print) | LCCN 2016036960 (ebook) | ISBN 9781493838868 (pbk.) | ISBN 9781480757813 (eBook)
Subjects: LCSH: Lewis and Clark Expedition (1804-1806)--Juvenile literature.
| West (U.S.)--Discovery and exploration--Juvenile literature. | West (U.S.)--Description and travel--Juvenile literature. | Lewis, Meriwether, 1774-1809--Juvenile literature. | Clark, William, 1770-1838--Juvenile literature. | Explorers--West (U.S.)--Biography--Juvenile literature.
Classification: LCC F592.7 .M85 2017 (print) | LCC F592.7 (ebook) | DDC 917.804/2--dc23
LC record available at https://lccn.loc.gov/2016034227

Teacher Created Materials
5301 Oceanus Drive
Huntington Beach, CA 92649-1030
http://www.tcmpub.com

ISBN 978-1-4938-3886-8

Printed by: 590835
Printed in: Taiwan

Table of Contents

The United States Doubles in Size

Thomas Jefferson became the third president in 1801. The country was much smaller then than it is today. It did not include any land west of the Mississippi River. Jefferson wanted to change this. He dreamed of the country stretching across the continent. In 1803, part of this dream came true.

Thomas Jefferson

France had a powerful leader named Napoleon Bonaparte (BOH-nuh-part). He wanted to make money for his country. So, he decided to sell some land.

Napoleon Bonaparte

France owned a huge piece of land called the Louisiana Territory. Napoleon said he would sell it to Jefferson. The Louisiana Purchase cost $15 million. For that, the United States got almost 828,000 square miles (2.1 million square kilometers) of land. Suddenly, the nation was twice as big!

Jefferson wanted to know all about these lands. So, he decided to send a group of men on an **expedition**. They would travel through the Louisiana Territory and write what they saw.

SIDE PROJECT

Jefferson had another job for the expedition team. He wanted them to find a river route from the Mississippi River to the Pacific Ocean called the **Northwest Passage**. He hoped this passage would help Americans trade furs.

Fur traders buy furs from American Indians in the late 1700s.

Preparing for the Journey

Jefferson knew just who he wanted to lead the trip. He had known Meriwether Lewis all his life. Their families lived near each other in Virginia. After serving in the army, Lewis became Jefferson's personal secretary. Jefferson liked that Lewis was brave, strong, and curious.

Meriwether Lewis

Lewis was happy to lead the expedition. He started choosing the rest of his **crew**. First, he asked an old army friend named William Clark to be his co-captain. Clark had a lot of experience traveling in the wilderness and along rivers and lakes.

Lewis did a lot of studying to get ready for the trip. Five different scientists taught him. He learned which plants and animals he could eat. He studied **navigation**, **surveying**, and American Indian history. The scientists also told Lewis what he should bring.

William Clark

Lewis headed towards St. Louis in 1803. He and Clark picked up a crew of about 45 men by the time they got there. They would later be called the **Corps** (KOHR) of Discovery. The men set up camp. Then, they spent months training.

telescope, peace medal, compass, and tomahawk

This is St. Louis, the starting point of the expedition.

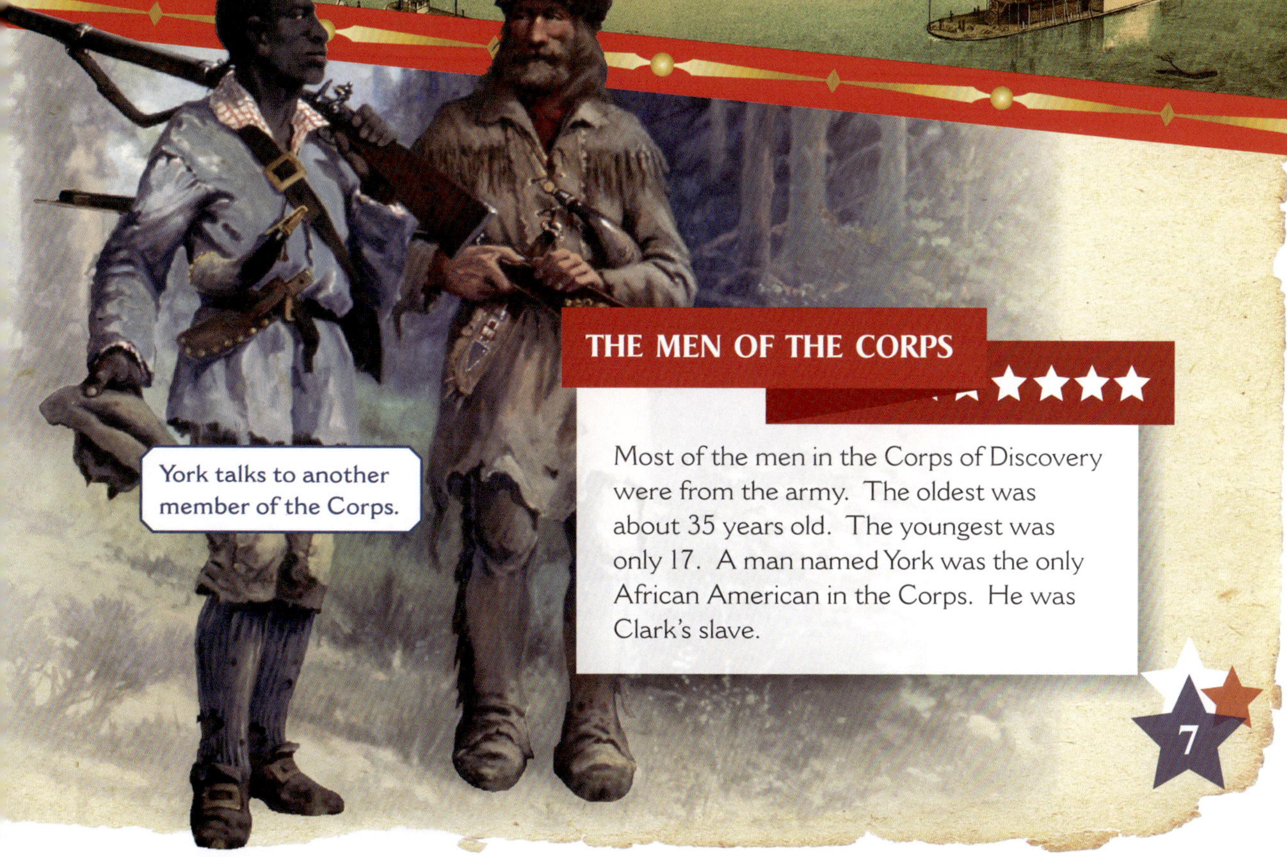

York talks to another member of the Corps.

THE MEN OF THE CORPS

Most of the men in the Corps of Discovery were from the army. The oldest was about 35 years old. The youngest was only 17. A man named York was the only African American in the Corps. He was Clark's slave.

Jefferson told Lewis that he wanted him to keep detailed notes during the trip. He asked Lewis to make copies of the **journals** just in case one was lost or destroyed. He even suggested making a copy on birch bark because it was more durable.

Jefferson didn't want the Corps to take any chances. He knew it might be dangerous in tribal land. He told Lewis to turn around and return home if they faced a battle with American Indians.

The plan was for the Corps to reach the West Coast. Once there, a merchant ship could bring them home. Jefferson even wrote a letter of credit. This letter said that the government would pay for their return.

Indian Presents

This is a list of items that Lewis and Clark bought to give as gifts to American Indians on their trip.

Clark's journal from the expedition

birch bark

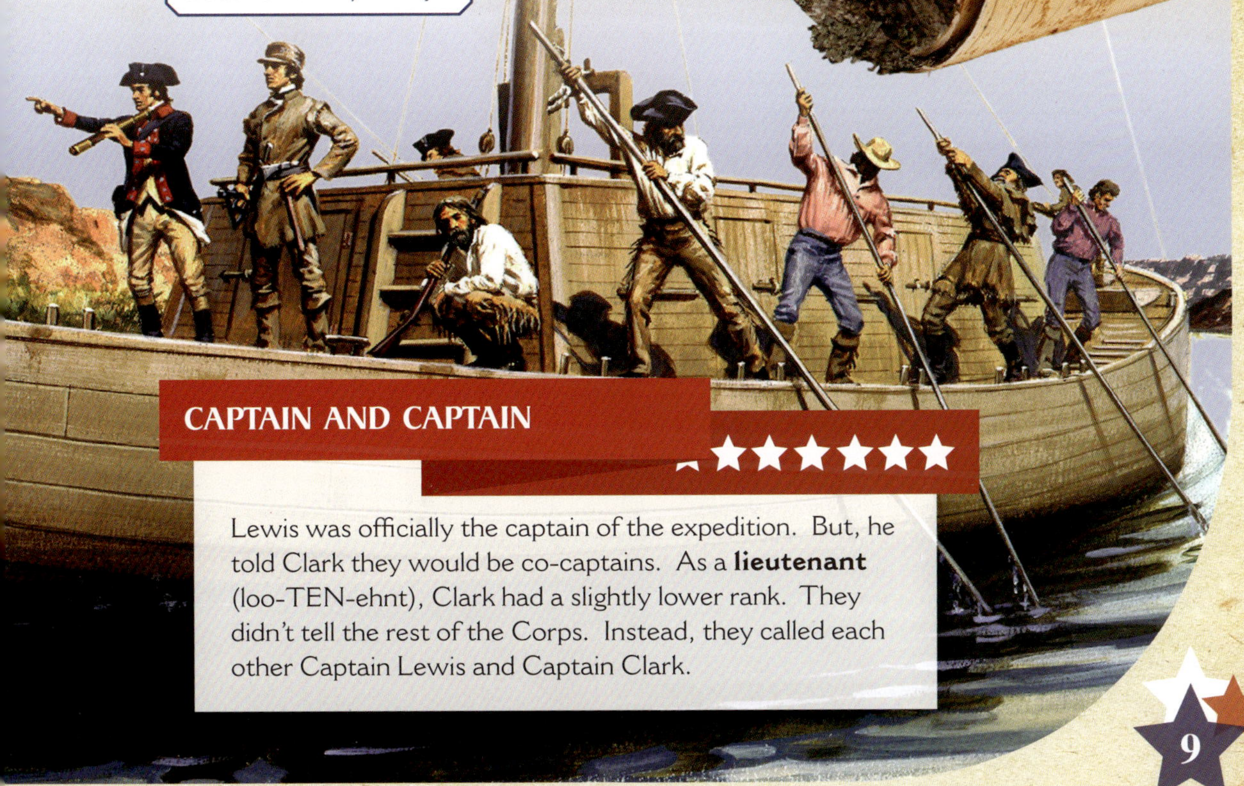

Lewis and Clark captain a boat on their journey.

CAPTAIN AND CAPTAIN

Lewis was officially the captain of the expedition. But, he told Clark they would be co-captains. As a **lieutenant** (loo-TEN-ehnt), Clark had a slightly lower rank. They didn't tell the rest of the Corps. Instead, they called each other Captain Lewis and Captain Clark.

The Journey Begins

The Corps of Discovery began its journey with about 45 men on May 14, 1804. The men left in three boats. One was a large wooden **keelboat**. It took 21 men to row it. The other two were smaller boats called **pirogues** (PEE-rohgs).

They planned to travel northwest along the Missouri River. This would lead them to the Rocky Mountains. There, they would cross a **pass** through the mountains. Rivers on the other side would take them to the Pacific Ocean.

Traveling upstream on the river was very hard. Tree branches and rocks often blocked the boats. Mosquitoes and ticks constantly bothered the men.

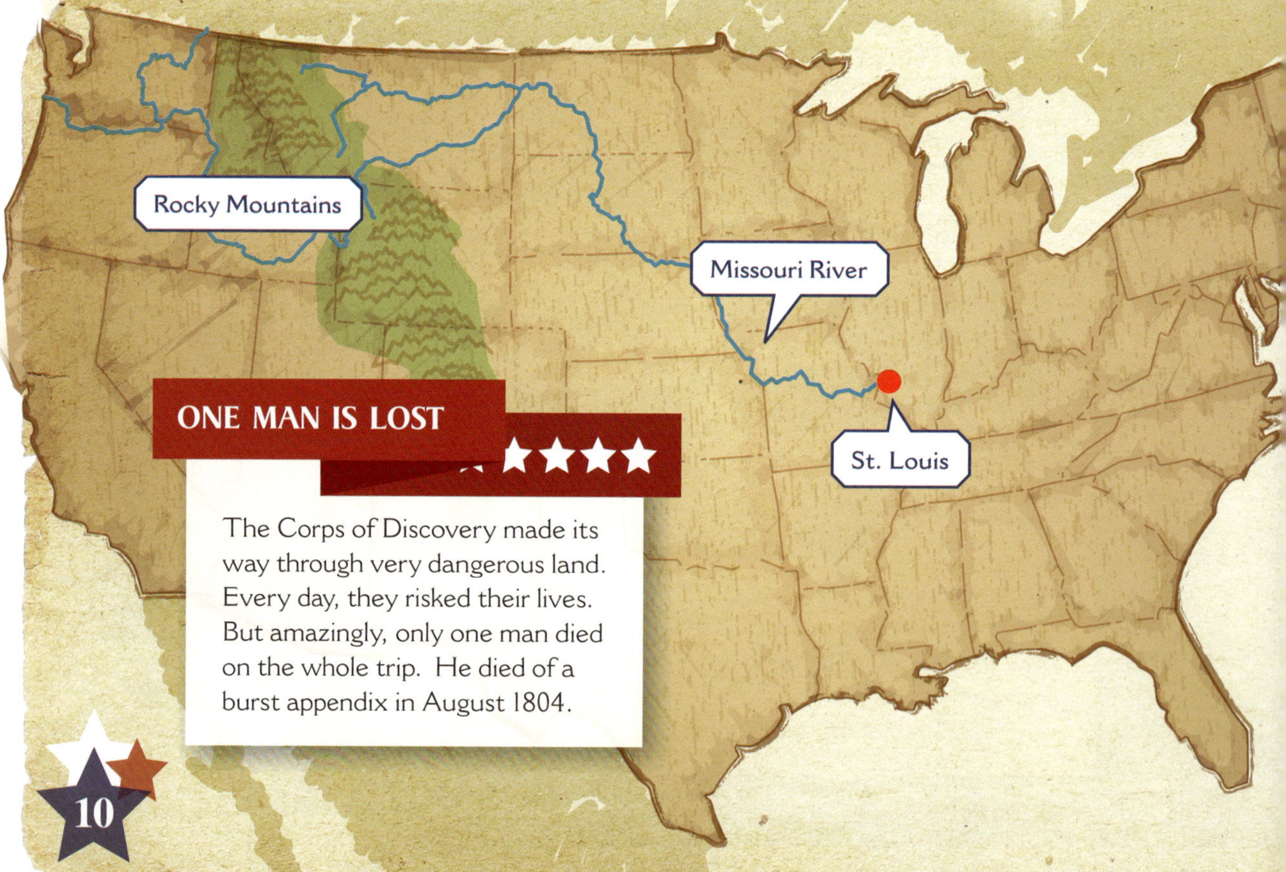

ONE MAN IS LOST

The Corps of Discovery made its way through very dangerous land. Every day, they risked their lives. But amazingly, only one man died on the whole trip. He died of a burst appendix in August 1804.

replica of a pirogue

Lewis was a good leader. The men respected and trusted him. But he was very serious and liked to be alone. Usually, he walked along the shore with his dog Seaman. Clark was more fun. He loved to talk and tell jokes. He was in charge of the boats.

Both captains kept journals during the expedition. They wrote about their adventures. They recorded the weather and made maps of the land and the water. They drew and described all the new plants and animals they saw. These included bison, coyotes, prairie dogs, and jackrabbits.

pages from Clark's journal

Jefferson had asked the men in the Corps to learn about American Indians in the West. Lewis planned to give them gifts. He hoped that would make them more friendly. He brought medals, beads, mirrors, brass buttons, tobacco, combs, and other items.

The Corps met their first American Indians in what is now Iowa. Most of them were friendly, but others were not so welcoming. One tribe thought they did not get enough gifts. They threatened to take one of Lewis and Clark's boats. The tribe aimed their arrows at the boat. The Corps pointed a gun right back at the tribe. Both groups were nervous. To everyone's relief, the tribe changed its mind.

Lewis and Clark meet an American Indian.

The crew reached what is now North Dakota in October. They made friends with the Mandan Indians. They decided to stay in one of their villages until spring. The Corps built a camp nearby and called it Fort Mandan.

The Corps hired a new member that winter named Toussaint Charbonneau (too-SAHN SHAR-boh-no). He was a fur trapper who lived with the Mandan people. He had a young Shoshone (shuh-SHO-nee) wife named Sacagawea. Sacagawea was pregnant with her son, Jean Baptiste (ZHAHN BAP-teest), at the time. Charbonneau and Sacagawea also joined the expedition.

Fort Mandan

CHECKING IN

Lewis and Clark were busy during the winter. They spent hours preparing reports and samples for President Jefferson. Then, they sent a boat back to St. Louis with all of the information.

This is the list of items that Lewis and Clark sent Jefferson from Fort Mandan.

Sacagawea Helps the Corps

Lewis and Clark allowed Charbonneau to bring his wife along. They hoped she would be able to help them. They were right!

Sacagawea was able to communicate with other American Indians. And the tribes trusted her. They thought a group that traveled with a woman and a baby would not be a threat.

When the Corps encountered Sacagawea's tribe, they sent a guide to help the Corps cross the Rocky Mountains. And her tribe sold horses cheaply to the Corps.

To arrange for this, she spoke to the chief. Communication took a long time. In these meetings, Lewis and Clark talked to another member of the Corps in English. He spoke to Charbonneau in French. Charbonneau spoke to Sacagawea in Hidatsa. Then, Sacagawea spoke to the chief in Shoshone. The communication reversed when the chief responded.

Sacagawea and her son

DR. LEWIS

While with the Mandan, Lewis and Clark acted as the village doctors. It was Lewis who helped Sacagawea give birth to her baby boy that winter.

Sacagawea translates for the Corps.

Crossing Rivers and Mountains

In April, the expedition set off again on the Missouri River. Their Mandan friends sang and danced in celebration. The Corps now had 33 people. Lewis and Clark had dismissed some of the men over the winter for misbehaving. A few others chose to leave. The Corps set off in two pirogues and six small canoes.

One day, a storm appeared suddenly. The water grew rough. One pirogue almost turned over. But, Sacagawea saved the day. She saw that important supplies were washing away. She calmly reached overboard to grab them.

In June, the group came to a **fork** in the river. They didn't know which way to go. Lewis and Clark studied the two rivers and decided which one to take. The rest of the Corps thought they were wrong, but they followed their leaders. Lewis and Clark were right! A few days later, they made it to the Great Falls of the Missouri River. Everyone was relieved.

The Corps could not take their boats up the huge waterfalls. So, they cut down trees to make wagons. They used the wagons to drag their boats over the land. It took about a month to go almost 18 mi. (29 km).

After the falls, the Corps returned to the river. As they climbed the mountains, traveling became very hard. The men were glad when they reached Sacagawea's Shoshone village. With her help, the Corps was able to buy some horses to carry supplies across the mountains.

This museum display shows how the Corps carried their boats over the land.

The Corps cross mountains in what is now Idaho.

NEW CANOES

The men couldn't bring any boats through the mountain pass. So, they had to make new canoes on the other side. The Nez Percé (PUHRS) tribe taught them how to cut down trees and carve out the insides until the logs were hollow. They called these *dugout canoes*.

The expedition started across the Rocky Mountain pass in September 1805. The men had never seen such large mountains. They didn't realize how long the crossing would take.

The Corps was not ready for how cold it would be, either. They struggled through snow and freezing rain. They could not hunt, and the group soon ran low on food. Sometimes, they had to shoot their own horses for food. Otherwise, they would have starved to death.

At last, the group made it to the other side of the Rockies. They built five new canoes and set off down the Snake River. The river was very fast. Some canoes tipped over in the rushing **rapids**.

Soon, the river grew wider, and the waters became calm. The men were finally able to fish and hunt. They ate until they felt strong again.

A Welcome Sight in Oregon

The Snake River led into a region called Oregon. Then, it flowed into the Columbia River. The men wondered if they would ever reach the end of their long journey.

On November 7, 1805, the group finally saw the view they wanted most of all. As the morning fog lifted, they thought they could see the Pacific Ocean in the distance. The men were thrilled. In his journal, Clark wrote, "Ocean in view! O! The joy!" But, they were actually still 20 mi. (32 km) from the ocean. They made it to the Pacific a few weeks later.

EXPLORING OREGON

The Pacific Northwest, including Oregon, was not yet part of the United States. It did not belong to any country. The members of the Corps of Discovery were the first white men to explore this area by land.

replica of Fort Clatsop

The Corps set to work building a camp. They called it Fort Clatsop after a nearby tribe. The men waited at the fort for four months in hopes that an American trade ship would sail by. They wanted to catch a ride home.

The Corps of Discovery rests and plans the next step of their journey.

The Long Trip Home

In the spring, the crew gave up on catching a ship home. On March 23, 1806, they began to head back by land. At first, they took the same route they did coming west. But after passing through the Rocky Mountains, the group split up to explore more land. Lewis traveled north up the unexplored Marias River. Clark returned by way of the Yellowstone River. The crews met up again at the Missouri River. Then, they continued along their original route.

The Corps stopped to visit their friends at the Mandan village. When it was time to go, Sacagawea and her family stayed behind. The crew was sad to say goodbye to her and her family. They owed much of their success to this brave Shoshone woman.

Sacagawea speaks with Lewis and Clark.

REMEMBERING A HERO

Nobody paid much attention to Sacagawea after the expedition. But in time, she became one of the most famous women in history. Sacagawea is honored by more statues than any other American woman. She was even put on a gold dollar coin in 2000.

The Corps of Discovery made it back to St. Louis on September 23, 1806. These brave men survived amazing challenges. They explored 7,689 mi. (12,400 km) of wilderness. Crowds cheered their arrival. The Corps had been gone almost two and a half years. After all that time, everyone thought they were dead.

Congress was happy with the Corps. They offered a bonus to the men. Lewis and Clark each received 1,600 acres of land for their roles. The other men were each given a 320-acre plot of land in the West. They were also paid twice as much as they expected.

statue of Lewis, Clark, and Seaman in Missouri

William Clark went on to live a long, happy life. He married and had children. When Clark heard a rumor that Sacagawea had died, he offered to adopt her two children. He died at the age of 68.

Meriwether Lewis had a hard time after the expedition. He had money problems and couldn't find a job he liked. He struggled with depression. Sadly, most historians think he took his own life in 1809.

Lewis and Clark

1814 map of Lewis and Clark's expedition

OVER BUDGET

When President Jefferson asked Congress to fund the expedition, he said it would cost $2,500. Lewis went a bit over budget. The trip ended up costing $38,722! That's equal to almost one million dollars in today's money.

An Open Door to the West

The Corps of Discovery learned that there was no direct water route from the Mississippi River to the Pacific Ocean. That was a disappointment. But in every other way, their expedition was a great success. Lewis and Clark's journals were full of useful information. They drew maps of the land and the rivers. They described 178 new plants and 122 new animals. The Corps explored the land of the Louisiana Purchase. Fur trappers, **mountaineers**, and settlers soon moved into this new land. Lewis and Clark also claimed the Pacific Northwest for the United States. Now, the country reached all the way to the Pacific Ocean.

This expedition began a time of great expansion for the United States. The country became larger and wealthier because of Lewis and Clark.

FROM FRIENDS TO ENEMIES

Lewis and Clark made friends with almost all the American Indian groups they encountered. But, soon, settlers began hunting and building homes on tribal lands. This led to many years of terrible fighting in the West.

American Indian camp in the Pacific Northwest

A group of settlers explores the land.

1804 map of the Louisiana Purchase

Network It!

If you were to take a journey to a place you have never been, how would you prepare? Who would you take with you? And how would you report your journey to the public on social media?

Plan your trip by listing your chosen crew along with reasons why you chose them. Then, make a list of the supplies you will need. Finally, create a plan to record your journey on some type of social media. Record at least three days of your journey, showing what you discovered.

3
5
track my journey
Like

Glossary

corps—an organized group of people involved in the same activity

crew—a group of people working together

expedition—a journey to a new place by a group of people for a specific reason

fork—a point where a river or a road splits in two or more directions

journals—books where people write about the things that happened during the day

keelboat—a boat with no sails that can carry a lot of goods

lieutenant—an officer in the army, navy, or air force with a rank below captain

mountaineers—people who explore, hunt, camp, and travel in the mountains

navigation—finding the best way to travel from one place to another place

Northwest Passage—a sea route connecting the Atlantic and Pacific Oceans along the northern coast of North America

pass—a route that goes through mountains, so you do not have to go around them

pirogues—small wooden boats like canoes

rapids—the dangerous parts of a river where the water moves very fast

surveying—using tools to measure and inspect an area of land

Index

Your Turn!

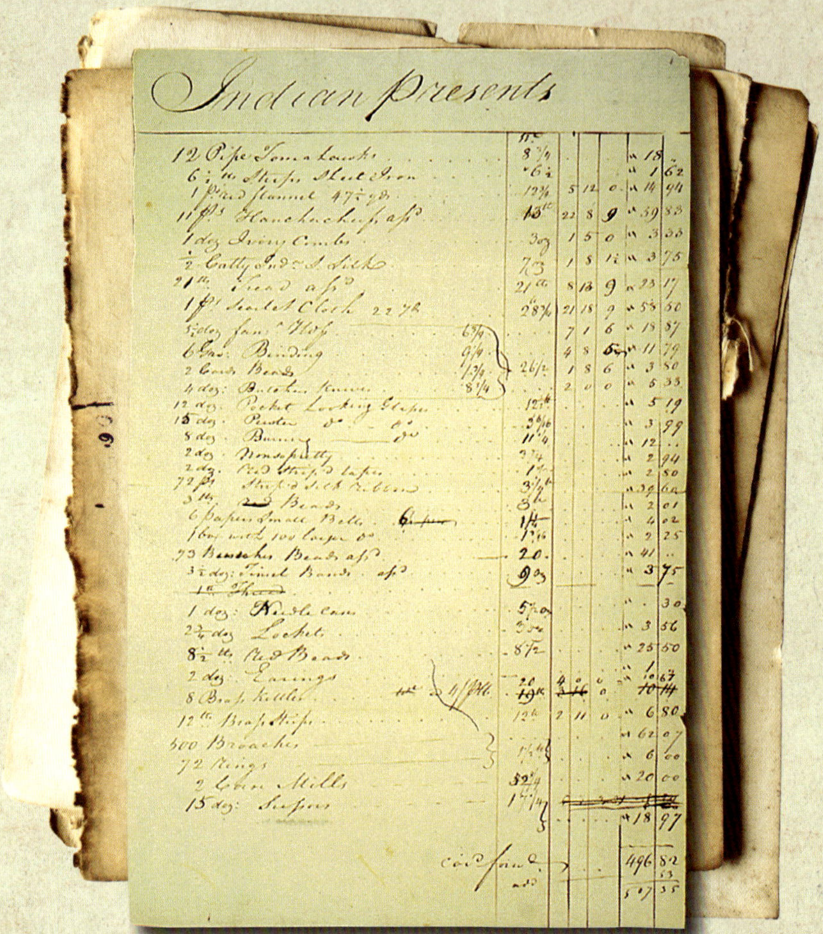
Indian Presents

A Gift for You

This page shows a list of items that Lewis and Clark took to give American Indians as gifts. If you were in charge, what would you have brought? Make a list of at least 10 items, and explain why they would be good gifts.